Self-criticism and the Imposter Syndrome

Ivan Salvaterra

Content:

Chapter 1
self-criticism,
a complex psychological process

Self-criticism is a complex psychological process that involves evaluating ourselves, our thoughts, feelings, and behaviors. It is a normal part of human life, but it can be both constructive and destructive.

Definition of self-criticism

Self-criticism can be defined as the process of evaluating our thoughts, feelings, and behaviors and coming to a conclusion about whether they are acceptable or not. It can be constructive when it helps us learn from our mistakes and improve as people, or destructive when it leads us to feel bad about ourselves and sabotage our own goals.

The role of self-criticism in personality development

Self-criticism is an important concept in personality psychology that refers to how people evaluate and judge themselves. According to theorists, our levels of self-criticism are closely linked to our personality traits and our psychological well-being.

Excessively self-critical people tend to score high on neuroticism on personality assessments. Neuroticism involves a chronic level of emotional instability and negative emotions. Self-critical people with high neuroticism often experience feelings of guilt, anxiety, sadness, and shame. They judge themselves harshly and feel like they constantly don't meet standards.

In contrast, people at the other end of the spectrum who lack appropriate levels of self-criticism tend to be low in neuroticism and high in narcissism. Although self-criticism can be harmful to health in extremes, a total lack of self-criticism leads to overconfidence, difficulty accepting responsibilities, and problems in relationships, reaching the typical case of the "pervert".

Finding the right balance of self-criticism requires self-awareness, self-compassion, and the ability to recognize areas of growth without becoming overwhelmed by feelings of inadequacy. With maturity comes a greater understanding of our strengths, limitations, and possibilities for positive change.

From a personality psychology perspective, developing a balanced, growth-oriented form of self-criticism is an important part of establishing stability, perspective, and direction in life. Excessive self-criticism is linked to mood disorders such as depression and anxiety, while an inability to honest self-reflection is associated with narcissism and related interpersonal problems. Our levels of self-criticism offer information about our mental health and our relationships.

Types of self-criticism

Self-criticism can be positive or negative, constructive or destructive.

Positive self-criticism: it is what helps us learn from our mistakes and improve as people. It allows us to identify our areas of improvement and take steps to correct them.

Negative self-criticism: it is what leads us to feel bad about ourselves and sabotage our own goals. It makes us focus on our flaws and prevents us from seeing our strengths.

Functions of self-criticism

Self-criticism can have several functions, including:

• **Self-regulation:** helps us control our behavior and avoid making mistakes.
• **Learning:** allows us to identify our areas of improvement and take measures to correct them.
• **Motivation:** it can drive us to achieve our goals.

Psychological consequences of self-criticism

Self-criticism can have positive or negative psychological consequences, depending on its type and function.

Positive consequences: positive self-criticism can help us:

• Increase our self-esteem.
• Improve our learning capacity.
• Achieve our objectives.

Negative consequences: negative self-criticism can lead us to:

•   Low self-esteem.
•   Depression.
•   Anxiety.
• Lack of confidence in ourselves.

The world of self-criticism

The process of self-criticism can have an adaptive or maladaptive nature and is related to perfectionism and self-esteem. Adaptive self-criticism involves an objective and constructive evaluation of oneself, which can contribute to personal growth. On the other hand, maladaptive self-criticism is associated with over-demand, guilt, and devaluation, which can negatively affect self-esteem and emotional well-being.

Psychotherapy is an area where self-criticism is worked on, since it seeks to increase the capacity for perception and reflection towards oneself, detecting and reinforcing functional behaviors, and modifying dysfunctional ones to increase control and adaptation to the environment.

Self-criticism, like perfectionism, can have its origins in early childhood, influenced by parenting patterns such as the demand for high levels of achievement and performance in children.

How you can develop constructive self-criticism

Constructive self-criticism is a skill that can be developed through practice and reflection. Some strategies to develop constructive self-criticism include:

• Be honest and objective when evaluating your actions, behaviors, and thoughts.
• Identify strengths and weaknesses, and work to improve them.
• Learn from mistakes and failures, instead of blaming or devaluing yourself.
• Be kind to yourself and recognize your achievements and efforts.
• Seek constructive feedback from trusted people.
• Practice meditation and mindfulness to increase self-awareness.
• Avoid over-demanding and excessive perfection, and accept that making mistakes is part of the learning process.

Ultimately, constructive self-criticism is a skill that can be developed through practice and reflection and can contribute to personal growth and informed decision-making.

What are the differences between constructive self-criticism and destructive self-criticism?

As we have said, self-criticism can be constructive or destructive, and the difference between the two lies in the feeling that is derived from them. Constructive self-criticism involves an objective and honest evaluation of oneself, to improve and grow personally, while destructive self-criticism manifests itself through guilt, anger, and devaluation, and can have negative effects on self-esteem and emotional well-being.

Constructive self-criticism focuses on improving attitudes and actions, and is not punitive, while destructive self-criticism focuses on pointing out what is wrong in oneself, and can have a contemptuous and tragic nature.

In this way, self-criticism can be constructive or destructive, and the difference between the two lies in the feeling that is derived from them. Constructive self-criticism involves an objective and honest evaluation of oneself, intending to improve and grow personally, while destructive self-criticism manifests itself through guilt, anger, and devaluation.

How you can identify destructive self-criticism in yourself

To identify it in yourself, you can observe the following signs:

• Frequent feelings of guilt and anger.

• Punish yourself for mistakes with minimal consequences.
• Generation of constant negative judgments about oneself.
• Contemptuous, tragic, and disapproving internal communication.
• Feeling of inability, uselessness, and uncertainty about oneself

It is important to be attentive to these signs to identify destructive self-criticism and look for strategies to transform it into more compassionate and constructive self-criticism.

What are the signs that you are being too hard on yourself?

Some signs that you are being too hard on yourself include:

• Psychologically punish yourself for minimal errors.
• Criticize yourself too much even after having corrected a mistake.
• Prioritize homework over personal care.
• Feel discomfort when faced with the error and live with negative thoughts and guilt for the errors.
• Blame oneself for things that do not depend on oneself.
• Feeling like you are failing even though things go well.
• See one's own mistakes as unforgivable, unlike the mistakes of others.

These signs may indicate excessive and maladaptive self-criticism, which can negatively affect self-esteem and emotional well-being.

How destructive self-criticism affects mental health

Destructive self-criticism can severely affect a person's mental health. Some negative mental health effects of destructive self-criticism include:

Insecurity: Destructive self-criticism can lead to feelings of insecurity and low self-esteem, which can affect the ability to make decisions and face challenges.

Depression and anxiety: Excessive negative thoughts and unsatisfied feelings, such as depression and anxiety, can be a consequence of destructive self-criticism.

Stress: Destructive self-criticism can generate large doses of stress, especially if the self-criticism is frequent and intense.

Deterioration in self-esteem: Destructive self-criticism can lead a person to a significant deterioration in their self-esteem, which can affect their ability to self-evaluate and self-appreciate.

Decreased motivation and energy: Destructive self-criticism can decrease motivation and energy, which can affect the ability to learn from situations and improve.

It is important to identify destructive self-criticism and seek strategies to transform it into more compassionate and constructive self-criticism, which can contribute to improving mental health and emotional well-being.

How destructive self-criticism can be treated in therapy?

Treating destructive self-criticism in therapy may involve a variety of strategies, including:

Self-observation and awareness: Identify and record self-critical thoughts to understand their origin and pattern.

Cognitive restructuring: Challenge and replace self-critical thoughts with more realistic and compassionate ones.

Mindfulness: Practicar la atención plena para observar los pensamientos autocríticos sin juzgar, lo que puede ayudar a reducir su impacto emocional.

Autocompasión: Fomentar la autocompasión y la amabilidad hacia uno mismo, en lugar de la autocrítica despiadada.

Identifying parenting patterns: Explore and understand how parenting patterns may have contributed to destructive self-criticism.

Psychotherapy techniques: Employ therapeutic approaches such as cognitive behavioral therapy, acceptance and commitment therapy, and schema therapy to address destructive self-criticism.

These strategies can be part of a comprehensive approach to treating destructive self-criticism in therapy, to promote more compassionate and healthy self-criticism.

What type of therapy is most effective to treat destructive self-criticism

There is no specific type of therapy that is most effective in treating destructive self-criticism, as treatment can vary depending on each person's individual needs and characteristics. However, some therapies that have been used to address destructive self-criticism include cognitive behavioral therapy, acceptance and commitment therapy, and schema therapy. A small approximation of them is below:

1. **Cognitive-behavioral therapy:** Cognitive-behavioral therapy (CBT) is a type of psychological therapy that focuses on the relationship between thoughts, feelings, and behaviors. Its goal is to help people identify and change negative thoughts and beliefs that contribute to their psychological problems.

CBT is based on the idea that thoughts, feelings, and behaviors influence each other. Negative thoughts can lead to negative feelings, which in turn can lead to negative behaviors. For example, a person who thinks "I'm not good enough" may feel anxious or depressed, which may lead them to avoid social situations.

CBT helps people identify their automatic thoughts, which are negative thoughts that occur quickly and unconsciously. Once people become aware of their automatic thoughts, they can begin to question and challenge them. Following the previous example, if a person thinks "I'm not good enough" they may begin to wonder if it is true or if there is another way to interpret the situation.

CBT also helps people develop coping skills. These skills may include relaxation, problem-solving, and time management.

CBT is an effective treatment for a wide range of psychological problems, including:

- Anxiety
- Depression
- Eating Disorders
- Obsessive-compulsive disorder (OCD)
- Post-traumatic stress disorder (PTSD)
- Personality disorders

CBT is usually done in individual sessions with a therapist. Sessions usually last between 50 and 60 minutes. The number of sessions necessary varies depending on the problem being treated.

CBT is an active therapy in which the patient actively participates in the treatment process. The therapist provides the patient with the necessary tools and support so that she can identify and change her negative thoughts and behaviors.

The benefits of CBT include:

- Improvement of psychological symptoms
- Improved quality of life
- Increased self-esteem
- Development of coping skills

CBT is a safe and effective treatment that can help people overcome a wide range of psychological problems.

2. Acceptance and Commitment Therapy: Acceptance and Commitment Therapy (ACT) is a type of third-generation psychological therapy that is based on relational framework theory. Relational framework theory maintains that language and cognition are relational processes that are learned through interaction with the environment.

The goal of ACT is to help people accept their internal experiences, both positive and negative, and commit to actions that are meaningful to them.

ACT focuses on six key processes:

• **Mindfulness:** Mindfulness is the ability to be present in the present moment, without judgment. ACT teaches people to develop mindfulness so they can observe their thoughts and feelings without identifying with them.

• **Cognitive defusion:** Cognitive defusion is the process of distancing oneself from thoughts and beliefs. ACT teaches people to see their thoughts as simple mental events, rather than facts.

• **Acceptance:** Acceptance is the process of allowing internal experiences, both positive and negative, to exist without trying to change them. ACT teaches people to accept their internal experiences, even if they are unpleasant or painful.

• **Values:** Values are principles that guide our actions. ACT helps people identify their values and commit to actions that are consistent with them.

• **Committed behavior:** Committed behavior is the action that a person takes based on their values. ACT helps people develop skills to take action, even when faced with challenges or obstacles.

ACT is effective in treating a wide range of psychological problems, including:

- Anxiety
- Depression
- Eating Disorders
- Obsessive-compulsive disorder (OCD)
- Post-traumatic stress disorder (PTSD)
- Personality disorders

ACT has also been used to treat physical problems, such as chronic pain and heart disease.

ACT is an active therapy in which the patient actively participates in the treatment process. The therapist provides the patient with the necessary tools and support so that she can develop the six key processes of ACT.

The benefits of ACT include:

- Improvement of psychological symptoms
- Improved quality of life
- Increased self-esteem
- Development of coping skills

3. Schema therapy: Schema therapy (ET) is a type of cognitive-behavioral therapy that focuses on helping people identify and change maladaptive schemas, which are negative beliefs and expectations about themselves, others, and the world.

Maladaptive schemas develop in childhood and adolescence as a result of negative or traumatic experiences. They can lead to a wide range of psychological problems, such as anxiety, depression, personality disorders, and addictions.

ET is based on the idea that maladaptive schemas are activated in stressful or challenging situations. When a maladaptive schema is activated, the person may experience a wide range of negative emotions, such as anger, fear, or sadness. These feelings can lead to negative behaviors, such as social isolation, substance abuse, or self-harm.

TE helps people identify and change their maladaptive schemas through a six-phase process:

Evaluation: The therapist helps the patient identify his or her maladaptive schemas. This is done through a combination of techniques, such as interviewing, testing, and story-telling.

Storytelling: The therapist helps the patient understand how his or her maladaptive schemas developed from her early experiences.

Evaluating the evidence: The therapist helps the patient evaluate the evidence that supports or refutes her maladaptive schemas.

Challenging schemas: The therapist helps the patient challenge her maladaptive schemas. This is done through a combination of techniques, such as cognitive restructuring, exposure, and practicing coping skills.

Integration of the modes: The therapist helps the patient to integrate the modes it, which are different emotional and cognitive states that arise from the maladaptive schemas of it.

Transition: The therapist helps the patient develop a plan to maintain her progress after treatment.

ET is an effective treatment for a wide range of psychological problems, including:

- Personality disorders
- Anxiety
- Depression
- Eating disorders
- Mood disorders

• Post-traumatic stress disorders

ET is an active treatment in which the patient actively participates in the treatment process. The therapist provides the patient with the necessary tools and support so that she can identify and change her maladaptive schemas.

The benefits of ET include:

• Improvement of psychological symptoms
• Improved quality of life
• Increased self-esteem
• Development of coping skills

These therapies can help identify and challenge self-critical thoughts, encourage self-compassion and self-kindness, and promote healthier, more constructive self-criticism.

What role do parents play in the development of self-criticism in children?

Parents play a fundamental role in the development of self-criticism in children. Experiences of demands or critical environments from parental figures can have a great impact on the child's thinking patterns, leading them to internalize critical, comparative, or disqualifying messages in a significant way.

The way parents provide feedback and criticism to their children can influence the formation of self-criticism. Constructive criticism and encouraging self-compassion are important for healthy emotional development

Likewise, parents' self-esteem also influences their children's self-esteem, since children tend to model their behavior and attitudes after the example of their parents.

The origins of self-esteem

Self-esteem, as a psychological concept, has its origins in the work of William James, a New York psychologist, who analyzed the phenomenon of self-esteem in his work "The Principles of Psychology" in 1890.

Since then, self-esteem has been an essential aspect of psychology, especially clinical psychology, and has given rise to various theories of psychopathology and human behavior.

The concept of self-esteem varies depending on the psychological paradigm that addresses it, such as psychoanalysis or behaviorism.

Self-esteem has been associated with conditions such as depression, eating disorders, personality disorders, anxiety, and social phobia.

Self-esteem in psychology is defined as the set of perceptions, thoughts, evaluations, feelings, and behavioral tendencies directed toward oneself.

It is the general sense that a person gives to his or her worth or worth based on his or her subjective view of value.

Contrary to popular thinking, self-esteem does not arise from evaluating ourselves positively in each situation, but from observing ourselves objectively and estimating and accepting our self-concept.

Self-esteem influences various aspects of daily life, such as motivation, performance, decision-making, interpersonal relationships, and emotional and physical well-being.

People with good self-esteem are less likely to experience high levels of anxiety, stress, or depression in their daily routines.

Furthermore, self-esteem affects daily life to the extent that a person takes care of themselves and feels self-respect.

If self-esteem is positive, physical, emotional, and mental well-being is prioritized, including regular exercise, healthy eating, adequate rest, and the pursuit of activities that provide pleasure and satisfaction.

On the other hand, low self-esteem can negatively affect daily life, as it can generate repressed emotions, distort communication with others and with the environment, and affect the experience of life.

It can also lead to a lack of personal care, neglect of obligations, and poor job performance.

Therefore, self-esteem is an important factor in daily life, as it influences the way we value and perceive ourselves, which in turn affects our motivation, performance, interpersonal relationships, and emotional and physical well-being.

How you can measure self-esteem

There are various ways to measure self-esteem, but one of the best-known tests is the Rosenberg Scale, which consists of ten questions that evaluate the value that a person has of themselves.

Another way to measure self-esteem is through observation of behavior since self-esteem influences the way a person behaves and relates to others.

Questionnaires and interviews can also be used to assess self-esteem, although it is important to keep in mind that self-esteem is a subjective construct and can vary over time.

In any case, measuring self-esteem is important to understand how a person values and how this influences their daily life and their emotional and physical well-being.

What factors influence self-esteem

Self-esteem is a complex concept that can be influenced by various factors. Some of the factors that influence self-esteem are:

The family or family nucleus: the upbringing received within the family nucleus is one of the elements that influence the development of a person's self-esteem, especially in their childhood and adolescence.

The social environment: relationships with peers, academic performance, physical appearance, use of social networks, and cultural influences, among others, can influence self-esteem.

Personal characteristics: personality, self-image, self-efficacy, self-confidence, self-assurance, feeling of belonging, feeling of competence, and feeling of personal worth, among others, are internal factors that influence self-esteem.

It is important to note that self-esteem does not arise from evaluating ourselves positively in each situation, but from observing ourselves objectively and estimating and accepting our self-concept. Self-esteem is a fundamental aspect of mental health and general well-being, and its understanding is crucial for a person's psychological and emotional well-being.

How to improve self-esteem

Various techniques and habits can help improve self-esteem. Some of them are:

• Identify the origin of low self-esteem and work on it.
• Speak with respect and affection to yourself.
• Measure criticism and quarantine negative thoughts.
• Set realistic and achievable goals.
• Don't compare yourself with others.
• Accept and forgive yourself.
• Make constructive criticism about yourself.
• Seek spaces for validation and emotional ventilation.
• Share anecdotes and socialize with others.
• Disconnect and reset in free and leisure time.
• Have small, achievable goals that can help you see progress.
• Accept the personal qualities that make us unique.
• Take responsibility for your own life.
• Remember and value achievements and successes.
• Avoid procrastination and perfectionism.
• Identify and work on addictions and other problems that affect self-esteem.

It is important to remember that self-esteem can vary throughout life and that it is possible to work on its development with the help of a professional.

Chapter 2
The origins of self-criticism

Self-criticism is a complex psychological process that develops throughout life. Factors that contribute to its development include:

Personality: People with a perfectionist or anxious personality tend to be more self-critical.

Family history: Those who were criticized or rejected by their parents or caregivers during childhood tend to be more self-critical.

Life experiences: people who have experienced failures or rejections tend to be more self-critical.

The Personality

Personality is a set of psychological characteristics that influence our thinking, behavior, and emotions. People with a perfectionist personality tend to be very demanding of themselves and others. They set high goals and punish themselves if they don't reach them.

There are also those with an anxious personality who tend to be self-critical. They constantly worry about what others think of them and are afraid of making mistakes.

Family history

The relationships we have with our parents or caregivers during childhood have a great influence on our emotional development. People who were criticized or rejected by their parents or caregivers tend to develop a negative self-image. They feel unworthy of love and approval and tend to punish themselves.

Life experiences

The failures and rejections we experience in life can also contribute to the development of self-criticism. When we feel frustrated, we feel bad about ourselves and blame ourselves for what happened. Rejection from others can also damage our self-esteem and lead us to be more self-critical.

The factors that contribute to the development of self-criticism are complex and vary from person to person. However, it is important to understand these factors to develop healthy self-criticism.

How childhood influences the development of self-criticism

According to studies, the roots of internal self-criticism are found in childhood and may be related to the demands of parents and influential figures in education.

Furthermore, self-image, self-esteem, and self-concept are forged during childhood and adolescence, and their development has effects on the person's adult life.

On the other hand, self-compassion is necessary for children to know how to love and respect themselves.

How self-criticism is formed

As we have mentioned, the main factors in the formation of a critical attitude towards oneself are Parents, education; social norms and cultural environment; personal experience, and character of a person.

Excessive self-criticism can occur in a person who grew up in a family of strict, hyper-controlling parents and who was often scolded and criticized as a child. Another option is for the child to grow up in a social group with strict rules and stereotypes, for example, religious ones. These children are likely to be excessively strict with themselves in the future.

Insufficient self-criticism depends on the same factors. If family relationships were permissive ("do what you want, but don't interfere"), then there may be a lack of self-control.

On the other hand, there are people of a certain type who are not critical enough of themselves. A good example is narcissists; since they feel that "they are always good at everything." Narcissists admire even those qualities and "achievements" of yours that are objectively very mediocre.

The level of self-criticism is also closely related to a person's tendency to attribute responsibility for events to themselves or others. This is called "locus of control."

A person with an external locus of control, who tends to shift responsibility to others, has reduced self-criticism. He explains his failures and mistakes to external circumstances: "They explained it to me poorly," and "the deadlines were not realistic."

People with an internal locus of control are not afraid to take responsibility. But they may have another problem: excessive self-criticism. They feel responsible even for situations that are beyond their control. For example, the company is experiencing massive layoffs and the department head blames himself for not standing up for his employees.

Therefore, the level of self-criticism depends both on education and environment and on the character and psychological characteristics of a person.

What activities can be done to encourage constructive self-criticism in children?

Various activities can be done to encourage constructive self-criticism in children. Some of them are:

Set an example: Parents should be an example of positive self-esteem for their children, telling their own stories of how they have overcome mistakes and failures.

Teach to manage frustration and criticism constructively: It is important to teach children to accept criticism and manage frustration constructively, seeking effective solutions for each situation.

Foster self-compassion: Self-compassion helps children learn to love and respect themselves, offering them protection from destructive self-criticism.

Teach to know themselves: It is essential to teach children to know themselves sincerely, accepting their abilities and mistakes.

Promote an environment in which healthy self-esteem is fostered: It is important to provide an environment in which healthy self-esteem is fostered and children are taught to handle frustration and criticism constructively.

Seek learning: When children make mistakes, help them identify what they could have done differently and how they could improve in the future.

Accept children as they are: Make children feel that they are loved unconditionally, without judging them for their mistakes

Change the way you see mistakes: Instead of treating mistakes as failure, teach them to see them as a way of learning and as part of life

Tolerate frustration: Accept that children experience frustration and disappointments, and teach them how to overcome and learn from them.

Give examples: Give examples of positive self-esteem for children by telling stories of successful people who have overcome mistakes and failures.

Teach to manage frustration and criticism constructively: Help children accept criticism and manage frustration constructively, seeking effective solutions for each situation.

How you can teach children to improve their skills

To teach children to improve their skills, the following activities can be carried out:

Encourage curiosity: Provide situations and experiences that trigger curiosity in children, helping them to actively explore and learn

Promote experimentation: Accompanying children in their attempts to experiment and try things, supporting them in the learning process through trial and error

Repeat and practice: Ensure that children have the opportunity to repeat and practice the skills they are learning, allowing them to refine their skills and improve their performance

Imitate and learn from others: Learn from and from everything in your immediate environment, including adults and other children

Teach to manage frustration and criticism constructively: Help children accept criticism and manage frustration constructively, seeking effective solutions for each situation.

Teach to know themselves: It is essential to teach children to know themselves honestly, accepting their abilities and mistakes.

Promote attachment and affectionate bond: Weaving a warm and close relationship between the child and the adult caregiver is essential for the emotional and social development of children.

Repeat and practice: Ensure that children have the opportunity to repeat and practice the skills they are learning, allowing them to refine their skills and improve their performance.

How you can encourage curiosity in children to improve their learning

To encourage curiosity in children and improve their learning, the following strategies can be applied:

Answer their questions: Stimulate curiosity by answering children's questions in a thoughtful and encouraging way

Stimulate their interests: Identify and participate in the child's interests, encouraging them to pursue activities and hobbies that attract their attention.

Encourage questioning: Encourage children to ask questions about the world around them

Provoke their curiosity: Pose tailored challenges on topics that are of interest to them or new to promote the learning of new knowledge.

These strategies will help stimulate curiosity in children, which in turn will enhance their desire to learn and improve their learning process.

Chapter 3
The effects of self-criticism in self-esteem

Self-criticism is the tendency to view oneself and one's actions in a negative light. When performing self-criticism, a person, first of all, looks for weaknesses, errors, and deficiencies in himself and in his behavior. Self-criticism is often expressed in self-deprecating phrases, for example: "I am mediocre", "something bad always happens to me", "everything always falls out of my hands", etc.

Researchers who study self-criticism have observed four aspects of this behavior in people:

• Severity towards oneself;
• Feelings of guilt or anger towards oneself;
• Feeling of worthlessness, perceiving oneself as a burden to others;
• Shame and reluctance to show weakness.

With self-criticism, all these feelings often merge and it is difficult to separate one from the other.

Psychologists do not deny that self-criticism can have a positive effect, promoting personal growth. However, there is research that links self-criticism with depression, loneliness, and self-harm. Some of them indicate that self-criticism contributes to eating disorders, increases the risk of substance abuse, and juvenile delinquency, deteriorates physical health, and is even a factor in suicidal behavior.

Psychologists divide self-criticism into appropriate (positive) and toxic (excessive). It is normal to be critical of yourself, it is a property of a healthy psyche. Adequate self-esteem is based on the skills of healthy self-analysis and self-criticism: an objective perception of oneself, of its positive and negative traits, helps a person to realize, correct deficiencies, and, ultimately, achieve his goal.

How to develop adequate self-esteem

Healthy self-criticism and self-esteem are closely related. People with low self-esteem are overly self-critical and unfair to themselves. Impaired criticality is considered a type of mental disorder. This is also one of the main signs of depression.

Excessive self-criticism is expressed in:

• Self-accusation – "It's all my fault";
• Labeled: "I can't believe how stupid I am";
• Self-doubt: "I just don't know how to make the right decisions";
• Devalue one's actions: "Anyone can do this, it's not difficult."

Both corrosive self-criticism and the complete absence of self-criticism equally negatively affect a person.

If the inner critic "goes too far," then the person:

• He only sees disadvantages in himself, only notices mistakes, and ignores his successes and positive qualities;
• Not sure of himself, dependent on the opinions of others;
• Is subject to self-harm, feelings of guilt, and anxiety;
• He procrastinates, puts things off, and subsequently self-flagellates himself because he never started them.

If self-criticism is not enough and a person does not analyze his actions at all, then:

• He has difficulties in relationships, conflicts, and misunderstandings with his loved ones;
• His behavior may be immoral or asocial;
• "Step on the same rake", repeat the same mistakes;
• He does not grow personally or in his career.

Self-doubt

Doubt is a subjective feeling that raises a question about one's abilities and potential for success in various areas of life. In general, self-doubt is the fear of being yourself, arising from doubts about one's competence.

Self-doubt goes hand in hand with low self-esteem, but there is a difference between the two. Uncertainty manifests itself in a specific way and refers to the confidence that a person has in his or her qualifications in various areas of life: work, personal relationships, etc. Self-esteem is a complex concept, a global opinion about oneself as an individual.

Uncertainty about the particular, if a person experiences it regularly, deals blow after blow to self-esteem and, in the end, can shake it greatly.

Self-doubt is also often confused with introversion. An introvert is a personality type proposed by Swiss psychiatrist Carl Jung to describe people who direct their life energy inward. They prefer to think separately from the outside world, immersing themselves in the inner world. But introversion is not necessarily a marker and, especially, it is not synonymous with uncertainty. German psychiatrist Karl Leonhard saw strength in this individualism. According to his interpretation, the introvert has clear values and is not afraid to oppose the environment, unlike the extrovert, whom Leonhard calls a conformist, susceptible to external influence.

Another phenomenon with which doubt is sometimes confused is social phobia. Social phobia is included in the International Classification of Diseases and is an anxiety disorder. People prone to it fear the attention of other people, public spaces, and large companies, sometimes to the point of panic attacks, and therefore avoid social situations. Social phobia is a medical diagnosis that is treatable.

People who doubt themselves tend to think that they have been given an unusual and unlucky ticket to reach this state. This is not true: everyone experiences this feeling in different life situations. It is natural to doubt yourself when starting new projects or in a highly competitive environment. But sometimes uncertainty becomes chronic and reduces the quality of life.

Signs of doubt

Every person who has experienced self-doubt has experienced the emotions, thoughts, and bodily reactions that accompany this condition.

External (bodily) signs

• Rapid heartbeat, redness or paleness of the face, irregular breathing when speaking.
• Slurred speech, chattering and losing the thread of the story, jerky movements: a conversational race, just to finish the speech faster.
• Hunched figure, unconscious desire to take up less space and be less noticeable.
• The phrases "I think", and "It seems to me": the person seems to apologize for being in their place.

Internal (mental, behavioral)

• Comparing yourself with others: for a person who lacks self-confidence, it almost always turns out that nothing is in their favor.
• Inability to say "no": it is easier for a person to accept a job that is a burden for him than to refuse.
• Minimizing his merits, and inability to accept praise.
• Transfer responsibility for your life to circumstances or other people.
• Avoidance of initiative and responsibility.
• Arrogance, which serves as a defense mechanism, helps reject others before they can reject him.
• Perfectionism: sometimes insecurity is well disguised, but it still reveals itself in the eternal search for unattainable perfection and hyper-control.

How does doubt arise?

The first environment in a person's life (family and school) has a great influence. Among the reasons rooted in childhood are:

Parenting strategies: emotional deprivation of parents, prohibitions, and restrictions, excessive criticism or overprotection.

Copy the behavioral stereotypes that the child observes around her: according to the theory of the American psychologist Albert Bandura, the lack of self-confidence of parents is often inherited.

Bullying: Peers can be quite harsh in their assessments and judgments.

Learned helplessness - psychologist Martin Seligman believed that weak abilities to control the outside world can arise due to insufficient elaboration of the action-consequence connection, which is often observed among children in orphanages.

Self-criticism and self-esteem

Self-criticism can have a significant impact on self-esteem. Self-esteem is the evaluation we make of ourselves, our thoughts, feelings, and behaviors. Healthy self-esteem allows us to feel good about ourselves and have confidence in our abilities.

Positive self-criticism can have a positive effect on self-esteem. It helps us identify our areas of improvement and take steps to correct them. This can help us feel more capable and confident.

Negative self-criticism, on the other hand, can hurt self-esteem. It makes us focus on our flaws and prevents us from seeing our strengths. This can lead to feelings of inadequacy, low self-esteem, and lack of self-confidence.

Specifically, negative self-criticism can have the following negative effects on self-esteem:

• It makes us feel bad about ourselves.
• It makes us feel inferior to others.
• It makes us feel guilty or ashamed.
• It makes it difficult for us to achieve our goals.
• It leads us to self-destructive behaviors, such as addiction or self-harm.

Therefore, self-criticism is a complex psychological process that can have both positive and negative effects on self-esteem. It is important to learn to use self-criticism constructively, so that it helps us improve as people, instead of sabotaging ourselves.

Some tips for developing healthy self-criticism:

• **Be realistic with expectations.** Do not set goals that are impossible to achieve.
• **Focus on strengths, not weaknesses.** We all have strengths and weaknesses. Focus on your strengths and work to improve your weaknesses.

• **Be kind to yourself. We all make mistakes.** Don't beat yourself up for your mistakes.
• **Seek support from others.** Talking to a friend, family member, or therapist can help you develop healthy self-criticism.

How to avoid self-criticism

To avoid self-criticism, it is essential to adopt a more flexible and understanding attitude towards yourself and others. Here are some recommendations to control negative self-criticism and not allow it to affect our self-esteem:

Be more flexible: Avoid using a dichotomous criterion (black or white) to evaluate reality or yourself. Trying to be more flexible with the world and people can help reduce self-criticism

Evaluate objectively: Constructive self-criticism allows us to evaluate both the positive and negative points of our thoughts or feelings and from that evaluation begin a learning process to improve

Accept mistakes and failures: It is important to remember that all human beings make mistakes and failures, and these do not define our personality or value as people. Accepting our mistakes and failures can help reduce self-criticism

Promote self-esteem: Self-esteem is essential to avoid negative self-criticism. Promoting self-esteem and self-care can help reduce self-criticism and improve our self-esteem.

How to differentiate constructive self-criticism from negative self-criticism

To differentiate constructive self-criticism from negative self-criticism, it is essential to analyze how self-criticism is carried out and how it is used in the evaluation of our actions and thoughts. Here are some key differences between both types of self-criticism:

Language: Constructive self-criticism uses descriptive and objective language, while negative self-criticism uses critical and judgmental language.

Attitude: Constructive self-criticism is based on a positive and understanding attitude, while negative self-criticism is based on a negative and biased attitude.

Flexibility: Constructive self-criticism allows for flexible and adaptable evaluation, while negative self-criticism tends to be rigidly structured.

Acceptance of errors: Constructive self-criticism allows us to accept errors and failures as part of the learning and growth process, while negative self-criticism tends to blame the person for their mistakes and failures.

Objectives: Constructive self-criticism seeks effective solutions and faces problems constructively, while negative self-criticism tends to focus on problems and negative behaviors without proposing solutions.

In short, constructive self-criticism allows us to evaluate and learn from our mistakes and failures objectively and comprehensively, while negative self-criticism tends to be critical, judgmental, and biased, which can negatively affect our self-esteem and inner well-being.

How to avoid negative self-criticism

To avoid negative self-criticism, it is important to develop the skill of identifying and challenging self-critical thoughts. Some strategies include:

Self-observation: Be attentive to self-critical thoughts and recognize their presence.

Questioning: Challenging the veracity of self-critical thoughts, questioning whether they are fair, accurate, and useful.

Change of perspective: Try to see the situation from a more objective and compassionate perspective.

Self-compassion: Cultivate self-compassion and self-kindness instead of resorting to self-criticism. Self-compassion involves treating yourself with respect and kindness, without self-mortification, excessive self-demands, or self-punishment for mistakes.

It is a concept related to emotional intelligence that involves the awareness that, as human beings, we have defects, deficits, or negative characteristics. Everyone makes mistakes sometimes.

Self-compassion seeks the happiness and well-being of the person, after accepting one's limitations. However, self-pity should not be confused with self-indulgence, which would imply victimization on the part of the person who does not consider himself capable of facing an adverse situation.

Solution Focus: Instead of focusing on mistakes, focus on finding solutions and learning from experiences.

These strategies can help transform negative self-criticism into constructive self-criticism, promoting personal growth and emotional well-being.

How to improve self-esteem through constructive self-criticism

To improve self-esteem through constructive self-criticism, it is important to adopt a compassionate and personal growth approach.

Some strategies include:

Understand the purpose of self-criticism: Recognize that constructive self-criticism seeks growth and learning, not personal devaluation.

Descriptive and non-judgmental language: Use descriptive language when evaluating errors, avoiding negative self-criticism that judges and blames.

Deal with mistakes constructively: See mistakes as opportunities for learning and growth, and look for solutions to improve in the future.

Cultivate understanding and kindness toward yourself, rather than resorting to negative self-criticism.

By applying these strategies, constructive self-criticism can contribute to the development of healthy self-esteem, promoting emotional well-being and personal growth.

Chapter 4
self-criticism
and psychological well-being

Self-criticism can also have a significant impact on psychological well-being. Psychological well-being is a state of balance and satisfaction with life. It is characterized by positive emotions and relationships, a sense of purpose, and a sense of general well-being. It helps us feel good about ourselves and achieve our goals. This can lead to greater happiness, life satisfaction, and a sense of accomplishment.

Negative self-criticism, on the other hand, can hurt psychological well-being. It makes us focus on our flaws and prevents us from seeing our strengths. This can lead to feelings of sadness, anxiety, depression, and low life satisfaction.

Specifically, negative self-criticism can have the following negative effects on psychological well-being:

• It makes us feel bad about ourselves.
• It makes us feel inferior to others.
• It makes us feel guilty or ashamed.
• It makes it difficult for us to achieve our goals.
• It leads us to self-destructive behaviors, such as addiction or self-harm.

Self-criticism is a complex psychological process that can have both positive and negative effects on psychological well-being. It is important to learn to use self-criticism constructively, so that it helps us improve as people, instead of sabotaging ourselves.

Self-criticism can negatively affect psychological well-being in several ways:

Affects self-esteem: Negative self-criticism can cause a decrease in self-esteem, which can lead to a feeling of worthlessness and lack of self-confidence.

It influences general well-being: Self-criticism can affect our emotional and physical health, as it can generate stress, anxiety and depression

Prevents progress: Negative self-criticism can paralyze our actions and decisions, making it difficult to progress toward our objectives and goals.

Affects the relationship with food: Self-criticism can influence our relationship with food, which can lead to self-sabotaging behaviors and health problems related to food.

To combat negative self-criticism and improve psychological well-being, it is important to:

• Be more flexible and not use a dichotomous criterion to evaluate reality or yourself

• Use strategies to silence self-criticism, such as breathing deeply and repeating positive affirmations

• Seek help from a therapist or support group to learn how to manage self-criticism

Some tips for developing healthy self-criticism:

Be realistic with expectations. Do not set goals that are impossible to achieve.

Focus on strengths, not weaknesses. We all have strengths and weaknesses. Focus on your strengths and work to improve your weaknesses.

Be kind to yourself. We all make mistakes. Don't beat yourself up for your mistakes.

Seek support from others. Talking to a friend, family member, or therapist can help you develop healthy self-criticism.

What consequences can self-criticism have on mental health in the short term?

Affects self-esteem and confidence: Excessive self-criticism can negatively affect self-esteem and self-confidence, which can lead to a feeling of worthlessness and lack of confidence in actions and decisions.

It influences general well-being: Self-criticism can affect our emotional and physical health, as it can generate stress, anxiety and depression

Prevents progress: Excessive self-criticism can paralyze our actions and decisions, making it difficult to move towards our objectives and goals.

Contributes to social isolation: Excessive self-criticism can lead to social isolation, which in turn can negatively affect our mental health.

How self-criticism can affect long-term mental health

Self-criticism can affect long-term mental health in a variety of ways, as evidenced by the following findings:

Relationship with mental disorders: Self-criticism has been linked to disorders such as depression, anxiety, suicide, and eating disorders

Impact on self-esteem and confidence: Excessive self-criticism can negatively impact self-esteem and confidence, which in turn can influence emotional and general well-being

Contribution to over-demanding and burnout: Self-criticism can be a contributing factor to personal over-demanding, burnout, and, in extreme cases, mental health disorders such as anxiety and depression

To mitigate these long-term negative effects, it is crucial to address self-criticism healthily, turning to self-care strategies and, if necessary, professional help. Reducing negative self-criticism and working to build healthy self-esteem is an effective way to improve psychological health and emotional well-being.

What is self-demand

Self-demand is a personality characteristic that refers to what we ask of ourselves, and is characterized by the objectives we set for ourselves in our lives and how we approach those objectives.

Self-demand can manifest itself in various ways, such as:

• Set extremely high standards for yourself in all areas of life

• Constant striving to perfect their actions and achievements, often ignoring their limitations

• Be critical of yourself in the face of errors and failures

• Set very high goals and base self-assessment on achieving or approaching those standards.

Self-demand can have negative consequences on mental health in the short and long term, such as:

• Increase anxiety and depression levels

• Affect interpersonal relationships due to rigidity and constant criticism

• Hinder creativity and innovation

• Contribute to the development of mental health disorders such as anxiety and depression

Consequently, self-demand is a personality characteristic that can negatively affect mental health in the short and long term. To improve long-term mental health, it is important to set realistic goals, accept mistakes and failures, practice self-compassion and self-esteem, be more flexible, and seek professional help if necessary.

What does excessive self-demand mean?

If a person is too demanding of himself, it means that he does not have self-confidence and does not like open manifestations of individual qualities.

He is ashamed of his imperfections hidden from the world, so he strives to achieve perfection in everything.

Let's look at this quality from both sides.

Those around you undoubtedly feel the influence of a demanding person. After all, your expectations for others are the same as those you apply to yourself, and because of this, misunderstandings and rejection often arise. And this hurts relationships with family and friends.

The demand, on the one hand, is useful for a person:

• A positive image of the individual is created;
• Maintains tone, effectively utilizes and replenishes resources;

• Opens opportunities for systematic growth and goal achievement.
• The other side reveals a demanding person's vulnerability to criticism and objections.
• When you fail and make mistakes, you experience them too much and often raise the bar, even though you can't reach it.

When expectations are not met, one begins to feel dissatisfaction, imposter syndrome, and increased anxiety. If you are pressured by negativity and internal obligations ("shoulds") for a long time, then there is a high probability of falling into depression.

Determine if you are too demanding of yourself

The requirements are too high if you notice these signs:

• Feeling ashamed when you remember mistakes, mistakes, failures;
• Feeling dissatisfied with the environment;
• Refusing when loved ones and colleagues offer help and are willing to work hard;
• Most desires are unattainable;
• Do you notice manifestations of perfectionism?
• Highlight mistakes, failures, imperfections;
• Having self-doubt;
• Fear of making a mistake and having others witness defects and weaknesses;
• You feel that the other person is capable of doing a better job (imposter syndrome).

Achieving perfection by demanding a lot from yourself is questionable. After all, each stage will require increasing efforts and resources. If you constantly pursue an ideal, you will suffer from physical and moral exhaustion.

What is the source of the problem?

In most cases, inadequate education is a source of excessive demands. When parents showed strict control, they demanded conformity to the ideal. Thus, the growth and development of this personality quality occurred.

Over time, this leads to the formation of black-and-white thinking in the child: if he achieves a result that is not ideal, then he faces failure. An adult continues to have stereotyped thinking and does not see details or atypical solutions, and this limits his growth and development.

When self-demand is at normal levels, this contributes to the successful development of the individual. When the requirements are excessive and inflated, the person works to exhaustion, hides their defects, and does not share their experiences.

And sometimes, when you see an ideal person, you may not even suspect how unhappy and workaholic he is, driven by the fear of making a mistake.

How to differentiate between constructive self-demand and ruthless self-demand

Self-demand can be constructive or ruthless, and can be differentiated as follows:

Constructive self-demand: Constructive self-demand focuses on setting realistic and achievable goals, and is used as a tool to improve and grow personally.

It is based on positive and constructive internal dialogue and is used to motivate yourself and achieve goals.

Ruthless Self-Demand: Ruthless self-demand focuses on setting extremely high, unattainable standards, and is used as a tool to constantly judge and criticize yourself.

It is based on negative and destructive self-talk and can lead to anxiety, depression, and other mental health problems.

To differentiate between constructive self-demand and ruthless self-demand, it is important to pay attention to how self-demand manifests itself in internal dialogue. Constructive self-demand focuses on personal growth and is used as a tool to motivate yourself and achieve realistic goals, while ruthless self-demand focuses on constantly judging and criticizing yourself, and can lead to mental health problems.

Chapter 5
Strategies
for healthy self-criticism

The positive impact of self-criticism lies in discarding ineffective strategies of thought and action, gaining motivation to rise to a new level, analyzing the potential and goals that one sets for oneself, and the ability to predict events. Self-criticism can also make a person more pleasant in terms of communication, increase his ability to correctly evaluate himself, and cultivate a respectful attitude toward others. Adequate self-esteem and appreciation of one's abilities open doors for the person to self-development and improvement of personality, quality of life, and professional results.

But, at the same time, psychology does not look favorably at excessive self-criticism, which is an independent quality. This can easily lead to loss of internal balance, discord with oneself, and disruption of harmony. If we talk about an ideal situation, then a self-critical person accepts himself, can rejoice at victories and successes, and analyzes failures to draw the correct conclusions and change his behavior. But if you examine each of your drawbacks too diligently, as if under a microscope, or tend to scold and scold yourself for a long time, there is nothing good in this.

The harmful effects of self-criticism certainly exist and manifest when its level increases. If taken to the maximum, it will instantly turn into self-flagellation, so a person not only destroys himself but degrades himself. As a result, self-esteem drops and self-doubt begins to appear; a person becomes indifferent and even apathetic, alienates people from him, and loses the ability to make decisions. And feelings of guilt, shame, and self-pity become chronic.

Therefore, we can draw an intermediate conclusion by highlighting the advantages and disadvantages of self-criticism.

Benefits of self-criticism:

• Opportunity for personal improvement
• An objective look at oneself
• Recognize own negative qualities and defects.
• The ability to draw conclusions and learn from mistakes.
• Ability to adjust actions.
• Motivation to achieve new goals.
• Greater courage and self-confidence.
• Cut self-confidence and the feeling of "I am always right"
• Cut narcissism
• Cultivate respect for others.
• The ability to admit one's own mistakes.

In learning, the ability to criticize oneself activates the desire to acquire new knowledge and avoid looking at things superficially. At work, it helps determine directions for career growth, adjust actions, and move up the career ladder.

In interpersonal interaction, self-criticism develops the skills of active listening and empathy, provides an incentive to perceive other points of view and become a more interesting interlocutor, as well as to make new friends. Finally, in family, friendship, and romantic relationships, self-criticism teaches a person to seek compromises, admit when they are wrong, and show sincere attention and care for others.

And if you're wondering what a lack of self-criticism can lead to, just counteract its benefits and the picture will become clear in no time.

Disadvantages of self-criticism:

• Self-humiliation and self-flagellation
• Decreased self-esteem and destruction of personality.
• Depression and unstable mental status.
• Lack of confidence in oneself and one's abilities.
• Apathy and inaction
• Inability to make decisions.
• Closeness and indifference
• Negative outlook on life and self.
• Inability to see one's strengths
• Excessive demands on oneself
• Deterioration in communication with other people.
• Feelings of guilt and susceptibility to manipulation.
• Lack of positive emotions.
• Development of mental disorders.

These deficiencies cannot be ruled out, but we repeat that only unhealthy self-criticism has this effect, intensified and taken to the absurd.

If you suddenly notice something similar in yourself, you can try to correct the condition yourself: focus on successes and achievements, and surround yourself with positive people. But when these methods fail to change your attitude towards yourself, it makes sense to seek help from a psychotherapist. A qualified and experienced specialist will help you develop new patterns of behavior, restore self-esteem, and get rid of such poisons as guilt, self-excavation, and devaluation of your personality.

If you identify as a self-critical person, there are some things you can do to develop healthier self-criticism.

1. Be aware of your thoughts and feelings

The first step to developing healthier self-criticism is to be aware of your thoughts and feelings. When you feel self-critical, ask yourself:

I'm thinking?
How do I feel?
Are these thoughts and feelings realistic?

2. Challenge your negative thoughts

Once you are aware of your negative thoughts, start challenging them. Ask yourself:

Is there evidence to support these thoughts?
Is there another way to interpret the situation?
Am I being too hard on myself?

3. Focus on your strengths

We all have strengths and weaknesses. It is important to focus on your strengths and work to improve your weaknesses.

What am I good at?
In what areas do I need help?

4. Be kind to yourself

We all make mistakes. It is important to be kind to yourself and forgive yourself for your mistakes.

5. Seek support from others

Talking to a friend, family member, or therapist can help you develop healthier self-criticism.

Train the mind with daily self-affirmations

Here are ten positive affirmations that can help you overcome negative self-criticism and increase motivation:

1. I am capable of achieving what I set out to do.
2. I accept myself as I am, with my strengths and weaknesses.
3. I allow myself to feel pleasant and unpleasant emotions because they are all part of the process and normality.

4. I listen to my body and my mind, and I hug myself.
5. I focus on my strengths and what I can do, instead of focusing on my weaknesses and what I can't do.
6. I allow myself to make mistakes because they are an opportunity to learn and grow.
7. I treat myself with kindness and compassion, as I would a close friend.
8. I focus on the present and what I can do right now, instead of worrying about the past or the future.
9. I allow myself to ask for help when I need it because we all need help at some point.
10. I give myself permission to rest and take care of myself because it is important for my well-being.

I hope these affirmations help you feel more motivated and overcome negative self-criticism. Cheer up!

Keep in mind that you can also keep a book of gratitude, habits, or goals. All of this will help you keep track of your goals and plan your life.

Chapter 6
Self-criticism as a tool
personal growth

Self-criticism is a personal growth tool that allows people to evaluate their actions, behaviors, and thoughts to identify areas for improvement and learn from their mistakes.

We know that, although it can be understood as a negative fact, self-criticism is essential for personal improvement.

Here are some key aspects of self-criticism as a personal growth tool:

Self-critical capacity: Self-critical capacity is essential for personal growth since it allows us to evaluate negative points, behaviors, and thoughts, which facilitates learning from mistakes and improving weaknesses.

Self-analysis: Self-criticism allows people to reflect on their actions and behaviors, evaluating whether they are aligned with their goals and identifying areas for growth

Reflective improvement: Self-criticism is crucial for reflective improvement, which involves accounting for actions and behaviors to identify areas for growth and make necessary changes.

Personal growth: Self-criticism is essential for personal growth, as it allows people to learn from their mistakes, correct or mitigate weaknesses, and take advantage of opportunities for learning and growth.

Responsibility: Self-criticism allows us to be responsible for our actions and mistakes, which allows us to know ourselves better and optimize our coexistence with other people.

However, it is important to approach self-criticism with an open mind and focus on personal growth rather than perfection.

Furthermore, it is essential to avoid pathological criticism and focus on finding solutions and alternatives for future occasions.

Self-criticism can be a powerful tool for personal growth. It helps us identify our areas of improvement and take steps to correct them. However, it is important to use self-criticism constructively, so that it helps us improve as people, instead of sabotaging ourselves.

Here are some ways to use self-criticism constructively:

- Use it to identify your areas of improvement.
- Set realistic goals to improve yourself.
- Be kind to yourself when you make mistakes.
- Focus on your strengths and work to improve your weaknesses.

How you can develop self-critical ability

To develop self-critical ability, several approaches and practical advice can be followed. Some recommendations include

Self-awareness: Be aware of when you are being self-critical and try to do it frequently and intentionally to exercise this ability.

Positive attitude: Differentiate positive self-criticism from negative self-criticism through a constructive attitude focused on improvement, instead of blaming and punishing oneself.

Behavior Description: Focus on accurately describing behaviors rather than focusing on personality traits or supposed essence.

Self-analysis: Develop the capacity for self-analysis to learn from mistakes, and correct weaknesses or inappropriate personality traits.

Analytical capacity: Process self-knowledge and recognize the successes and mistakes made, analyzing one's situations, behaviors, actions, and thoughts.

Be clear that the purpose is to improve: Make sure that self-criticism is done to improve and learn, rather than blaming and punishing yourself.

Be relaxed: Choose a suitable time to carry out self-criticism, where you can be relaxed and focused on the process.

These strategies and tips can help strengthen self-criticism, allowing for more constructive reflection aimed at personal growth.

How to criticize yourself correctly?

The main and, perhaps, the most correct formula of self-criticism is expressed as "more - less - more." This means that if you manage to do something, great! But if the attempt was unsuccessful or you made a mistake, you need to admit it, reconsider, draw conclusions, and do it right next time.

In general, to be able to criticize yourself adequately, it is best to have a scale formed from your values and beliefs. It is also necessary to have a healthy lifestyle. A reasonable and objectively self-critical person knows what is important to him and can determine what traits and qualities he needs. After all, this is what helps to find the right direction for self-development. In this case, self-criticism will be reasonable, it will become a good support and will serve as an incentive to improve yourself and achieve success.

To develop constructive self-criticism, we advise you to accept that there are no ideal people in the world, not to become obsessed with the desire to always be right, but also not to back down when you are objectively sure of the correctness of your position. You must develop intuition and listen to it, learn to enjoy life, and not lose your sense of humor.

But let's talk more specifically about tips that will help you develop good internal self-criticism:

Be honest with yourself

Self-criticism is, above all, honesty and openness towards oneself. You can fool anyone, but not yourself, and there is no point in trying to disguise something, hide it, or justify yourself. By learning to tell the truth about yourself, you will take a big step forward and turn your conscience into that inner observer that will limit you in unwanted words, actions, and deeds.

Don't despise yourself

No mistake, stumble or failure is worth it for you to stop respecting yourself and start hating yourself. Self-criticism is self-development and you must understand that you need to work on yourself without feeling like a useless or worthless person. It is important to understand that you are not criticizing yourself as a person, but rather your wrong actions, misconceptions, opinions, and points of view. You must learn every day, and extract valuable experience from everything that works and what doesn't work. Mistakes are part of the life of each of us, but they are not a reason to destroy our inner world.

Curb your ego

Every action has a reason and can be both positive and negative. Let's not delve into examples, but let's take the simplest one: you can treat someone favorably, but what is the reason? Are you doing this just for fun or do you want to get some benefit for yourself? People often act based on selfish goals. Try to "catch" yourself in such actions and resort to self-criticism. Otherwise, you may succumb to self-deception, thinking that you are a good person when in reality you are someone who only loves yourself. By working on your ego and reducing it, you will become more critical of yourself.

Embrace your pride
Pride, like most others, is good in moderation. If it goes out of scale, a person immediately begins to defend himself even from harmless attacks in his direction. Pride can say that we are always right and not give other opinions the right to exist. Because of this, it is difficult to objectively evaluate yourself and understand the true reasons for your actions. If we "lower our nose a little", we will see ourselves from the outside and the fact that those around us do not wish us harm and do not want to offend us. Furthermore, this will allow us to be on the same level as other people and begin to show them more respect, and the latter, as we have already said, is a quality inherent in self-critical people. But there is no need to lose pride, because its absence, like the absence of self-criticism, only makes things worse.

Don't blame yourself
Criticizing yourself correctly is not easy, but it makes us move forward. Therefore, let's talk about balance again: you need to analyze your actions, but at the same time not feel excessive guilt. Sometimes it is useful to understand that you are to blame: it is a manifestation of conscience. However, if guilt hangs like a weight around the neck, it leads to self-criticism and a state of unhappiness. What's done, life doesn't stop and you too must move forward. To do this, you must realize where you went wrong and focus on doing the right thing.

Be wiser

You have decided to develop self-criticism. Your behavior has started to change, you pay attention to your mistakes and do everything you can to prevent them from happening again in the future. You have become a better person. But now your acquaintances, relatives, and friends behave completely differently, than they were used to, and a feeling of internal protest begins to take over you. And here it is very important to understand that there is no point in opposing other people (and vice versa). Nobody owes you anything, that's one thing, each one lives as they see fit, there are two of them, and each one is in their stage of development and formation. Instead of dissatisfaction, resentment, or anger, show wisdom: act as your instinct tells you and show others by your example how harmonious and developing a person you are.

Listen to people

It is not always possible for a person to be able to independently see where he is wrong. But those close by can see it. Competent self-criticism is also the ability to constructively perceive criticism from others. And you must develop it in yourself in every possible way, because only then will it have a positive effect on your personal growth. It is not always the case that when they tell you that you are doing something wrong they want to insult you or belittle your dignity. Many people wish him well and want him to become a better person. The sooner you learn to respond appropriately to comments from others, the faster work on yourself will produce results.

Criticize yourself out loud

This is a very useful and effective technique, in one way or another related to everything we have already said. If you suddenly did something wrong or acted recklessly, don't be afraid to admit it to other people in a clear voice. The benefit of this is, first of all, that reasonable people who are around will not only understand you but will also help you understand where exactly the mistake was made and how to correct it. Second, when your behavior upsets someone or disappoints them, self-criticism out loud will let that person know that you are admitting your mistake and asking for forgiveness. They probably won't accuse him of anything additional either. But here it is worth saying that this technique should be used only with those who have a positive attitude towards you, otherwise, your confessions will serve as a weapon that the enemy will be able to successfully use to your advantage.

Always try to remember that your task is to learn to reflect and be honest with yourself to reach a new level of yourself, being able to overcome your weaknesses, misconceptions, and prejudices. Self-criticism serves as the main goal of self-evaluation and the ability to see one's positive qualities and advantages over other people.

If you want to progress, you need to learn how to criticize yourself correctly. As a famous proverb says: "We see a speck in someone else's eye, but we do not notice a log in our own," and this is very reminiscent of human behavior. So, self-criticism is the right way to learn from mistakes, achieve mutual understanding in communication, establish harmony within oneself, and improve the quality of life.

What are the obstacles to developing self-critical capacity?

Several obstacles can hinder the development of self-critical ability. Some of them are
1
Fear of failure: Fear of failure can prevent people from critically evaluating themselves, as they fear facing their weaknesses and mistakes.

Low self-esteem: Low self-esteem can cause people to criticize themselves excessively and negatively, instead of focusing on personal improvement and growth.

Lack of self-awareness: Lack of self-awareness can prevent people from recognizing their weaknesses and mistakes, hindering the ability to learn and improve.

Defensive attitude: A defensive attitude can prevent people from accepting constructive criticism and closing themselves off from the possibility of learning and growing.

Lack of practice: Self-critical ability requires practice and constant effort, so lack of practice can impede its development.

It is important to recognize these obstacles and work to overcome them to develop a healthy and effective self-criticism capacity.

How to work on self-criticism in children

Working on self-criticism in children can be a challenge, but several strategies can help combat this tendency. Some of these strategies include:

Establish a rule at home: Explain to children that no one has permission to be cruel to another person, not even to themselves. This gives them a chance to tame the harsh words and, over time, they turn into more positive thoughts.

Naming the Inner Critic: Name the inner critic and help children get used to saying, "Oh yeah, that's how the monster would talk. But that's not me." This makes criticism much less powerful when confronted.

Work on emotional intelligence: Learn to say "I feel frustrated" (or disappointed, embarrassed, etc.) and help children find words to describe their feelings. This allows them to defend themselves to others and demand that people treat them with respect.

Shaping self-compassion: When children make mistakes, they should be made to recognize their limitations clearly, but without sending the message that self-criticism is an appropriate response to a mistake. This can improve your social-emotional skills throughout life.

Artistic activities: Use artistic activities as a way to work with your inner critic. This can help children express their emotions and thoughts in healthier ways.

Mindfulness Training: Participate in mindfulness training programs, such as Ready4Routines, which focuses on developing executive function skills for both parent and child in the context of building family routines. These programs can help children improve their social-emotional skills and handle self-criticism more healthily.

Chapter 7
Imposter syndrome

Imposter syndrome: How to overcome the feeling of fraud?

Imposter syndrome is a psychological phenomenon in which people who have achieved notable success feel inadequate, undeserving, or deceptive. Despite their achievements, these people feel that they are not competent and that their successes are simply the product of luck, deception, or favoritism.

Imposter syndrome is a relatively common phenomenon, affecting people of all ages, genders, and education levels. It is estimated that it affects 70% of people at some point in their lives.

People who suffer from impostor syndrome usually present the following symptoms:

- Feeling of not being good enough
- Fear of being discovered as impostor
- Avoidance of challenging tasks or situations
- Low self-esteem
- Anxiety
- Depression

Impostor syndrome can hurt the lives of people who suffer from it. It can make it difficult for them to achieve their goals, develop their careers, and enjoy their relationships.

This phenomenon affects people of different professions and levels of responsibility, especially women and those who are in positions of great responsibility.

At the same time, it is a mistake to believe that self-doubt and, especially, imposter syndrome are inherent only to "mere mortals." Celebrities also encounter them, and not just at the beginning of their trip. Natalie Portman, speaking to Harvard students as a 2015 psychology graduate, told them that she did not realize her accomplishments: "Twelve years after graduation, I must admit that I still do not feel my worth. I have to remind myself that I'm here for a reason. Today I feel the same as when I started at Harvard in 1999. Then it seemed to me that there was some kind of mistake: I wasn't smart enough to be here, and every time I opened my mouth I had to prove that I wasn't just a stupid actress. Sometimes uncertainty and inexperience can cause you to strive to meet the standards and expectations set by other people. But you can use your lack of experience to forge your path, one that is not dictated by others, but determined by you."

The American writer and Pulitzer Prize winner John Steinbeck wrote in his diary: "I am not a writer. "I am fooling myself and those around me." After finishing work on the novel "The Grapes of Wrath," which earned him an award, he said: "Sometimes I think I have done something worthwhile, but when the work is done, it turns into mediocrity." .

Michelangelo and Leonardo Da Vinci doubted his abilities. The latter is credited with the phrase "Tell me, did I manage to do something?" Vincent Van Gogh, according to his contemporaries, constantly suffered from self-doubt, but once said: "If you hear a voice inside you telling you that you cannot paint, do it by any means and the voice will be silent." The great Argentine writer Jorge Luis Borges found it difficult to finish a book since once finished, he did not stop correcting it again and again until he said Enough!

Insecurity in personal relationships

Insecurity in personal life manifests itself in the fact that a person questions his ability to please someone. At the beginning of a new relationship, you may feel afraid that the person you are close to will "notice" your flaws and feel disappointed. In existing relationships, this means violation of one's needs because it will be more convenient for someone, jealousy, and sometimes an endless transfer of one's anxieties and doubts to one's partner.

Some key aspects that contribute to the rise of imposter syndrome include:

• High and constant pressure for performance and image, which increases lack of self-confidence and generates constant doubts.

• The lower representation of women in management positions, can cause those who occupy them to feel more pressure.

• Stereotypes established in society that can affect the perception of people who suffer from it.

• Imposter syndrome can be an overwhelming feeling and make people who experience it feel isolated.

• Some people who suffer from it may express doubts about their abilities and believe that they are not enough.

• This disorder can affect people's work lives, as they may have difficulty making important decisions or taking advantage of new opportunities.

What causes imposter syndrome?

The factors that contribute to the development of imposter syndrome are complex and vary from person to person. However, some of the most common factors include:

Personality: People with a perfectionist or anxious personality are more likely to suffer from imposter syndrome.

Family history: People who were criticized or rejected by their parents or caregivers during childhood are more likely to develop a negative self-image.

Life experiences: People who have experienced failures or rejection are more likely to suffer from imposter syndrome.

How to overcome imposter syndrome

If you think you may be suffering from imposter syndrome, there are a few things you can do to overcome it:

One of the most important things you can do to overcome it is to recognize your achievements. Take some time to think about everything you have accomplished in your life. Have you received praise from your co-workers, teachers, or clients? Have you achieved goals that seemed impossible to you? By recognizing your achievements, you will begin to realize that you are capable of many things.

Facing your negative thoughts: One of the characteristics of imposter syndrome is the tendency to have negative thoughts about yourself. These thoughts can be very harmful, as they can lead us to doubt our abilities and sabotage our successes.

One way to overcome negative thoughts is to challenge them. When you have a negative thought, ask yourself:

Is there evidence to support this thinking?
Is there another way to interpret the situation?
Am I being too hard on myself?

Focus on your strengths: We all have strengths and weaknesses. It is important to focus on our strengths and work to improve our weaknesses. When you feel insecure about your abilities, remember your strengths. What am I doing well? What have others told you that you are good at?

Be kind to yourself: We all make mistakes. It is important to be kind to yourself and forgive yourself for your mistakes. When you make a mistake, don't beat yourself up. Learn from your mistakes and move on.

Seek support: Talking to a friend, family member, or therapist can help you overcome imposter syndrome. A supportive person can help you recognize your accomplishments, challenge your negative thoughts, and be kind to yourself.

If you think you may be suffering from imposter syndrome, you're not alone. Many people suffer from it and there are many things you can do to overcome it.

How to act in the workplace

• Create psychotherapy or job coaching programs that encourage people to recognize their value and get ahead.

• Promote collaborative workspaces where trust and security can be developed.

• Recognize both your own and other people's achievements and offer constructive feedback to everyone on a team.

• Promote diverse, equitable, and inclusive practices at work

What are the symptoms of impostor syndrome?

Symptoms of imposter syndrome include:

• Belief of not deserving one's achievements, attributing them to luck or the help of others.
• Disbelief in one's abilities.
• Constant fear of being discovered as a fraud.
• Expectations of failure in common situations of success or excellent performance.
• Demotivation associated with lack of personal confidence.
• Anxiety, sadness, depression, and fear of not having tried hard enough.

In addition, other signs can be observed such as a lack of self-confidence, downplaying achievements, fear or fear of failure, and burnout due to overwork.

These symptoms can manifest in different areas, such as academic, work, social, interpersonal, and family.

If you identify with several of these symptoms, it is important to seek psychological support to address imposter syndrome.

Imposter syndrome can affect professional self-esteem in a variety of ways. Sufferers often underestimate their achievements and avoid taking risks, which can lead to a lack of confidence at work and a constant feeling of dissatisfaction. Additionally, they may fall into patterns of procrastination or perfectionism to avoid being discovered as "frauds." All of this can cause decreased productivity and low self-esteem when it comes to your work skills. This insecurity can translate into a lack of confidence when presenting or sharing work, contributing to a decrease in self-esteem in public or work environments.

To overcome this syndrome, it is suggested to look for strategies to combat it, such as self-knowledge and awareness, and recognize achievements. Challenge negative thoughts, set realistic goals, and seek support from trusted friends, family, or colleagues.

What is strategic brief therapy and how it can help treat impostor syndrome

Brief Strategic Therapy is a therapeutic approach that focuses on solving problems effectively and quickly. It may be useful in treating imposter syndrome, as it focuses on identifying and modifying the beliefs and thinking patterns that underlie this disorder.

This therapy helps people identify and change underlying negative beliefs, develop new coping strategies, and recognize their value as a person.

Brief Strategic Therapy is effective in solving imposter syndrome by applying to the patient a set of stratagems that follow the logic of paradox and the logic of self-deception to solve the problem.

The duration of the therapy can be several sessions, but in general, it is an approach that seeks to solve the problem in a short time. Brief strategic therapy can help identify and modify the beliefs and thinking patterns that underlie this disorder, and provide strategies for recognizing one's value as a person.

How to overcome self-doubt

Doubt is a reversible process if you start working with it. Obsessive thoughts about one's inadequacy must be compensated for with new positive attitudes and thinking techniques. At the same time, getting rid of uncertainty doesn't go away in a couple of weeks: it's a long job.

The following steps are suggested:
Formulate and write down your positive qualities and strengths without touching on your achievements:
This is necessary for a person to develop the understanding that there are qualities in themselves that make people love them, regardless of their achievements or wealth.

Replace self-criticism with self-validation:
When a person lacks self-confidence, he is more sensitive to mistakes and failures, sometimes imaginary.

Validation is normalization:
It is necessary to remember that all people make mistakes, this is normal and appropriate. Self-criticism in this case is a useless thing that does not help in any way, it simply generates a lot of thoughts of "why am I bad?", but not a single one about how to improve.

Replace the concept of "mistake" with the phrase "growth zone":
Lack of experience or skill is not a reason for self-flagellation, because "I have discovered my growth zone and therefore I can work in it."

Don't be egocentric:
Insecure people tend to be very self-centered when looking for reasons for failure. There is no such thing as an entire situation that goes down the drain just because of one person. It is necessary to force thinking

not to follow the beaten path of finding who to blame but to look more broadly.

To experience:
People with low self-confidence often avoid trying something for fear of not succeeding. But when a person refuses to act, he receives a reinforcement of his insecurity, because he remains there. Trying is always 50/50. If successful, this may be the first boost of confidence.

Write down achievements and congratulate yourself:
This is an advanced level. People who lack self-confidence tend to devalue their achievements. You need to focus on the moments when something works and praise yourself, instill in yourself the idea that this success is not an accident, but the result of the efforts made.

Give yourself time:
Uncertainty did not appear in a day, week, or month; It was formed and consolidated over the years. To establish a new way of thinking, it is also necessary to carefully create a habit. It is important to be persistent in regularly using the techniques described and not expect quick results.

Don't focus on the bad:
Don't think that if something doesn't work, nothing will work out.

Pay attention to the body:
The human brain correlates directly with the body: it sends signals to it and collects information from it. The

more a person reflects and maintains an uncertain stance, the deeper they can become stuck in this state. It makes sense to go in the opposite direction and work on posture, self-presentation, and voice. The quicker you can get out of a posture of uncertainty, the easier it will be to let go of this feeling. Acting, singing or dancing courses can help with this.

In short, imposter syndrome is a psychological disorder that can affect people of different professions and levels of responsibility, especially women and those in positions of great responsibility. To prevent and overcome this syndrome, it is important to recognize it in time, seek psychological support if necessary, create psychotherapy or job coaching programs, promote collaborative workspaces, and recognize both your achievements and those of others.

#######